WASHINGTON, D.C.

FROM THE AIR

WASHINGTON, D.C.

FROM THE AIR

STEPHEN SMALL & MILLICENT JONES

THUNDER BAY
P·R·E·S·S

Published in the United States by
Thunder Bay Press
An imprint of the Advantage Publishers Group
5880 Oberlin Drive
San Diego, CA 92121-4794
www.advantagebooksonline.com

Produced by PRC Publishing Ltd
Kiln House, 210 New Kings Road
London SW6 4NZ

© 2000 PRC Publishing Ltd

The publisher would like to thank Tom Wood for taking all the photographs in this book and
Alexander D. Mitchell IV for his editorial assistance.

ISBN 1 57145 277 X

Library of Congress Cataloging-in-Publication Data available upon request.

Printed and bound in Italy

1 2 3 4 5 00 01 02 03

INTRODUCTION

Washington, D.C. is one of the most visited capital cities in the world. Each year over 20 million people descend on the seat of government to explore its historic landmarks, extraordinary museums, and charming neighborhoods. The appeal is an obvious one. If power can exist in a physical space, it exists here on a grand scale. In the Capitol building, the White House, and the Mall, Washington boasts the most potent symbols of political power in the world's most powerful nation.

But the city's monumental qualities (and above all else, Washington is about monumentalism) conceal a city of moderate size. This unique "state" is only America's 16th largest city, with a population of around 609,000—and this is also part of Washington's appeal. For all its wide vistas, inspired geometry, and classical architecture, Washington remains, in many ways, a small city that can be enjoyed on foot.

The city was not always so popular amongst visitors. Charles Dickens, visiting the city in the mid-1800s, described it as "a place of spacious avenues that begin in nothing and lead nowhere; streets a mile long that want only houses, roads, and inhabitants, public buildings that need but a public to be complete." The area that was to become home to one of the world's most powerful governments was initially populated by wealthy landowners who operated large, prosperous tobacco estates. These estates depended on the labor of African slaves, who were, in fact, the majority population in the area at the time.

When, in 1790, the Continental Congress authorized the selection of a new site for a permanent seat of government, the choice of location was not easy. Philadelphia had been the first capital of the new nation, which then moved for a short time to overcrowded Princeton, New Jersey. In deciding on a permanent location, there was great friction between leaders from the North and South, with threats from the South to secede if they were not happy with the new capital. After much debate, in January 1791 President George Washington chose the 100 square miles of land, which now comprises the District of Columbia, as well as a small tract across the Potomac River in Virginia.

Washington then made the fateful decision to appoint Frenchman Pierre Charles L'Enfant—a military engineer and architect whose father was an esteemed gardener at the court of Versailles—as Washington's chief city planner. L'Enfant can be credited with creating the backbone of the city as it appears today, with great diagonal areas crossed by a rectangular network of streets. L'Enfant's circles, which provide vistas in three directions, were clearly inspired by the gardens at Versailles.

Those who owned land in the District were not impressed with L'Enfant and his grand vistas. George Washington had originally persuaded landowners to sell their lots at $66 per acre, but they were to receive no compensation for public highways. When the property owners learned that L'Enfant's avenues were to be 160 feet wide and that of the 6,111 acres designated for the new capital, 3,606 were to be highways, they were vehemently opposed to the plan, as they would be forced to give so much of their property away.

Despite the unpopularity of his vision, L'Enfant would not be moved by commercial considerations. In fact, he refused to turn over his plan when it came time to sell the city lots, resolving to do nothing to help "speculators to purchase the best locations in his vistas and architectural squares and raise huddles of shanties which would permanently disfigure" his metropolis. The final straw came when one prominent landowner's new house obscured one of L'Enfant's great vistas. L'Enfant ordered it to be demolished immediately, and then was promptly fired. He was to die in obscurity, never seeing the beautiful city he so bravely imagined.

As the century began in 1800, the fledgling nation moved its government to its new home in Washington. A member of the cabinet, Secretary of the Treasury Wolcott, was less than enthusiastic about the place as he found it:

"There are few houses in any one place, and most of them small, miserable huts, which present an awful contrast to the public buildings. The people are poor, and as far as I can judge, they live like fishes, by eating each other. You may look in almost any direction, over an extent of ground nearly as large as the city of New York, without seeing a fence or any object except brick-kilns and temporary huts for laborers."

When the British attacked the city in 1812 and tried to burn it to the ground, they were cheered on by the locals, who were tired of the squalid living conditions. After the Civil War, it was difficult to attract civil servants to the city, as it harbored outbreaks of malaria and yellow fever.

It was only in the late 1800s, that the city began to fulfill L'Enfant's vision of a majestic capital that would be envy of others throughout the world. After $4 million bond issue was approved by Congress, City Boss Alexander Shepard embarked upon a project to rebuild the city's infrastructure, providing paved streets, sewers, a decent water supply, gas lines, and row upon row of the trees that it is now so famous for. The work was expensive—Shepard ended up spending $18 million on the improvements and eventually fled from the wrath of an angry government to early retirement in Mexico.

Michigan Senator James McMillan drafted a plan to continue the beautification of the city in 1902. The Lincoln Memorial and the Washington Monument, as well as most of the Greek and Roman inspired architecture found in the city were built during this period at a cost of around $60 million. The city continued its transformation, remaking itself in the Beaux-Arts tradition given prominence at the Chicago Colombian Exhibition.

Washington, D.C. today is home to many of the nation's great libraries, medical research centers, art galleries, and the nation's number one visitor attraction (surpassing even Disneyland!), the Smithsonian Institute. An eclectic array of cultural traditions, from Dim Sum to Duke Ellington, can be found in its 120 diverse neighborhoods. Many of the great symbols of American political and social history are represented here—from the original Star Spangled Banner to the Emancipation Proclamation.

These symbols are a powerful reminder that this great city has served as a symbol of democracy since its creation. All who visit it are invited to experience the glory of its public buildings, parks, and monuments. Join us as we embark on our flight over the city.

Looking across Washington, D.C. from just south of the Capitol to the northeast at dusk. In this photograph can be seen the Department of Transportation—the distinctive square building constructed around a cross—and beside it is the Department for Housing and Urban Development. Above that, running up toward the Washington Monument is the Mall, lined either side by some of the most famous galleries and museums in the world, including the perfectly circular Hirshhorn Museum.

Taken from the northwest and looking southeast over the city this photograph shows an enclave of governmental buildings close to the Mall. At the intersection of 12th Street and Pennsylvania Avenue to the right of the photograph and embraced by the red-roofed federal triangle, lies the Old Post Office building, built in 1899 and conspicuous with its tall clock tower. The *New York Times* declared the building "a cross between a cathedral and a cotton mill." After only ten years, demands for its destruction were heard and in 1914 the Post Office was moved to a different location: this site then became known as the "Old" Post Office. The building re-opened in the mid-1980s as a center for entertainment, restaurants, and shopping.

The Old Executive Office Building is shown to the left of center of this photo. It was completed in 1888 and was designed to house the State, Navy, and War departments. The building came to be seen as inefficient and was nearly demolished in 1957. Since 1981, major renovations have been carried out including the development of a comprehensive preservation program and the formulation of a master plan for the building's continued use. The various agencies that comprise the Executive Office of the President, such as the Office of the Vice President, the Office of Management and Budget, and the National Security Council are still housed here. To the left of the photograph can, again, be seen the red roofs of the Federal Triangle and behind them the National Museum of American History with the towers of the Smithsonian in the background. Directly behind the monument are the U.S. Holocaust Memorial Museum and the Bureau of Engraving and Printing. The Francis Case Memorial Bridge can be seen linking the southwest of the city to East Potomac Park. The water to the right of the bridge is a corner of the Tidal Basin where tourists can hire paddle boats to get a beautiful view of the Thomas Jefferson Memorial, the F.D.R. Memorial, and the cherry trees that surround them.

The vista from the Federal Center Southeast over the confluence of the Anacostia and Potomac rivers. Fort McNair, with its National War College, lies at the mouth of the Washington Channel and above it can be seen a thin strip of trees marking Hains Point, the southern tip of East Potomac Park. The Anacostia is spanned by the Frederick Douglas Memorial Bridge, which carries South Capitol Street across to the south bank, where it is flanked by Anacostia and the Anacostia Naval Station.

The lights of America's capital illuminate the city's grand boulevards and two of the nation's most recognizable landmarks—the Washington Monument and the Capitol Building. At the top of the monument two red beacons mark its position to air traffic.

The Jefferson Building of the Library of Congress (center with dome) celebrated its centennial in 2000. It is the world's largest library, containing over 115 million books, films, photographs, prints, maps, sound recordings, musical scores, and digital materials. The Library's mission is "to sustain and preserve a universal collection of knowledge and creativity for future generations." To its left is the Supreme Court, standing on the site of the "Old Brick Capitol" that once served as the nation's capitol and, later, as a Civil War prison.

In these photographs of the Washington Mall as it stretches from the Capitol Building to the Washington Monument to the Lincoln Memorial, it is easy to see the grandeur of the city's master plan. George Washington commissioned Major Pierre Charles L'Enfant to design the city in 1792. L'Enfant designed a grid system interposed with wide streets, circles, and squares with radials slashed across, in a design inspired by his native Paris. Fortunately, Congress never permitted any high-rise buildings to obscure the grandness of the city's original layout. The Capitol itself is located at the eastern end of the Mall on a plateau 88 feet above the level of the Potomac River, commanding a westward view across the Capitol Reflecting Pool to the Washington Monument and the Lincoln Memorial. The site, originally called Jenkins' Hill, was in L'Enfant's words, "a pedestal waiting for a monument."

Initially, much of L'Enfant's original plan was ignored, allowing for unregulated development, which marred the dramatic vista between the Capitol and the Washington Monument. A park commission was organized under the auspices of Senator James McMillan to prepare a design that would revitalize the neglected Mall. In the foreground of the photograph, to the left, is the roof of the Supreme Court Building; to the right are the Senate Office Buildings.

The Capitol Building is one of the most architecturally impressive and symbolically important buildings in the world. For nearly 200 years it has been home to the meeting chambers of the Senate and the House of Representatives. Begun in 1793, the Capitol has been built, burned, rebuilt, extended, and restored; today, it stands as a monument to the American people and their government.

A great example of 19th century neoclassical architecture, the design of the Capitol was derived from ancient Greece and Rome. It reflects the ideas that influenced the nation's founders as they framed their new republic. As the building was expanded from its original design, harmony with the existing portions was carefully maintained.

Originally a wooded wilderness, the U.S. Capitol grounds today provide a park-like setting.
Over 100 varieties of trees and bushes are planted around the building and thousands of
flowers are used in seasonal displays. The grounds were designed by Frederick Law
Olmsted, who planned the expansion and landscaping of the area that was performed
from 1874 to 1892. Also seen in the photograph are the Senate Office Buildings between the
Capitol and Union Station.

In this photograph, taken from the south of the Mall, are some of America's finest museums. Stretching out along the north of the Mall is the National Museum of Natural History, which is dedicated to furthering an understanding of the natural world and whose exhibits include a butterfly garden as well as the famous dinosaur hall. Opposite are the towers of the Smithsonian Institution, which was founded in 1846 with $550,000 bequeathed to the United States by English scientist James Smithson "for the increase and diffusion of knowledge." The first of what would become over a dozen Smithsonian buildings scattered across the Mall and Washington, the red sandstone "castle" was designed by James Renwick, Jr. The Smithsonian Institution is today the world's largest museum complex and even houses the tomb of its founder. To the right of the Smithsonian is the circular Hirshhorn Museum and Sculpture Garden and behind the Natural History Museum can be seen the distinctive buildings of the Federal Triangle.

With two wings separated by 4th Street on the National Mall, the National Gallery was created by Congress in 1937. The paintings and works of sculpture given by Andrew Mellon, its founding patron, formed the nucleus around which the collection has grown. It is divided into the West Building and the East Building designed by I.M. Pei. The most famous feature of the latter, not seen in this early morning photograph, is the sharp angle of the southwest corner that has been rounded by thousands of visitors touching the wall.

In the center of this photo you can see the National Museum of American History, located at 14th Street and Constitution Avenue. The museum's collection includes George Washington's field tent, the original Star Spangled Banner, and the ruby slippers from *The Wizard of Oz*. The present Beaux-Arts-style building was completed in 1964.

The Bureau of Engraving and Printing has been printing America's paper money since 1914. Today, the bureau produces over nine billion federal reserve notes each year—about $538 million per day—as well as 20 billion postage stamps, military certificates, and presidential invitations from three sites, two of which are located in Washington (the third is in Fort Worth). The present building was built during the 1930s.

The Washington Monument stands as a tribute to the nation's first president. The notion of such a tribute was first raised just following the American Revolution of 1776, but it was over 100 years before the monument finally took shape. In 1833, the Washington National Monument Society was formed to raise funds for the building project. Each American was to be asked to donate no more than a single dollar. The original plans for the monument, drawn up by Robert Mills, called for an obelisk to be surrounded by a Greek temple with niches for statues of prominent Americans. The monument was to be crowned by Washington in a toga, commanding a chariot. The cornerstone of the monument was laid in 1848 by President Polk. However, interest in the project began to decline soon after and funds grew scarce in the 25 years which followed. Construction stopped when only 156 feet of the 500-foot obelisk was completed and was finally resumed in 1876 when the government resolved to take over the project. The grand plans for a temple surrounding the obelisk were abandoned in favor of the simple obelisk which now stands. On December 6, 1884, a 3,300 pound marble capstone was set on the obelisk and topped with a nine-inch pyramid of cast aluminum, a rare metal at the time. The monument was dedicated on February 21, 1885, and officially opened to the public in October 1888.

The Washington Monument is now visited by over 3,000 people per day and has been the site for many protest marches and demonstrations in the last century. On August 28, 1963, over 200,000 men and women assembled here for the March on Washington and made their way to the Lincoln Memorial to hear Dr. Martin Luther King Jr. give his inspiring "I Have A Dream" speech. In the years 1967 through 1973, more than a dozen anti-Vietnam War demonstrations took place on the grounds. Above is a photograph of the Washington Monument as seen through the elegant Colorado marble columns of the Lincoln Memorial.

This photo shows the reflecting pool across from the Vietnam Veterans Memorial, where the Korean War Veterans Memorial is located. The memorial, unveiled in 1995, depicts soldiers in full battle dress approaching an American flag and commemorates the sacrifice of all those who fought to defend South Korea. An etched granite mural runs alongside the group of figures.

Since being transferred to the National Park Service in 1933, the National Mall has served as an open space for celebrations, demonstrations, protests, festivals, and numerous recreational activities. This photograph shows the view from west to east across the Lincoln Memorial and the reflecting pool to the Washington Memorial.

The view over the Lincoln Memorial to north Washington. On the horizon to the right can be seen the Shrine of the Immaculate Conception (see page 98). In 1911, Congress authorized the building of the Lincoln Memorial and construction took place between 1914 and 1922. Architect Henry Bacon modeled his design for the building after the Greek Parthenon. Built into the design are symbols of Union: the 36 exterior Doric columns represent the 36 states in the Union at the time of Lincoln's death.

This view shows the extensive grounds around the Washington Monument and Lincoln Memorial. Bounded on the north by Constitution Avenue and on the south by the Tidal Basin the park has many other monuments, including one on an island in the lake seen to the left of the reflecting pool to the those who signed the Declaration of Independence.

The memorial is now a central part of any tourist's trip to Washington, and is widely considered to be a fitting testimonial to one of the greatest leaders of the United States. However, this was not always so. The design was much criticized at the time of building for not reflecting Lincoln's humble ideals and background.

IN THIS TEMPLE
AS IN THE HEARTS OF THE PEOPLE
FOR WHOM HE SAVED THE UNION
THE MEMORY OF ABRAHAM LINCOLN
IS ENSHRINED FOREVER

Lincoln was dubbed "Savior of the Union" for the leadership he showed during the Civil War. This statue was created by Daniel Chester French, the leading American sculptor of his time. The face of the statue is based on a mask of Lincoln's face taken during the Civil War and reflects the tribulations he faced. The imposing figure is composed of 28 blocks of white Georgia marble, joined together so precisely that the seams are barely visible.

"The Awakening" sculpture by J. Seward Johnson, Jr. is a 70 foot giant dramatically rising from the earth at Hains Point in East Potomac Park. The artist spent much of his life as a painter before turning his talent to sculpture in 1968. His pieces—most famous of which are life-sized bronze figures of people in public places, such as reading on a park bench—now adorn cities all over the American continent.

The view from over the Tidal Basin to northwest Washington from above the Jefferson Memorial. The city's low-level building policy allows a panoramic vista, and even the National Cathedral can be seen on the horizon to the left. To the left of the photograph the Kutz Bridge is visible.

Among the cherry trees that surround the Tidal Basin is the Franklin Delano Roosevelt Memorial. Dedicated by President Clinton in 1997 it is a tribute to one of the nation's finest leaders, who guided the U.S. through the Great Depression and World War II, and had an unprecentented 12 years in office.

In 1934, Congress authorized the creation of a memorial to Thomas Jefferson, one of the great founders of the nation. The design of the memorial, by architect John Russell Pope, is based on the Roman Pantheon, a building with a style much favored by Jefferson as evidenced by his home at Monticello. The memorial stands amid the Tidal Basin, famous for the cherry blossom trees which bloom there for just two weeks every year.

1600 Pennsylvania Avenue is now visited by over a million people each year. However, the city at the time of the White House's completion was quite different from the modern urban metropolis of today. Abigail Adams complained about her new home: "We have not the least fence, yard, or other convenience without, and the great unfinished audience-room (the present East Room) I make a drying-room of, to hang the clothes in."

The building was burned by British Troops during the War of 1812. Interior damage to the house was repaired, but the exterior walls were colored black due to fire damage. After being painted white, the building became known as the "White House," a name Congress made official in 1902. The architecture of the exterior remains much like it was when it was originally built. The interior, however, has been completely renovated over the years, with each president giving it his unique stamp. Andrew Jackson installed indoor plumbing, Harry Truman added a porch, and Bill Clinton, in an effort to stay fit, initiated construction of an indoor-running track.

The south lawn of the White House, the oldest public building in Washington, looking over Constitution Avenue and the Ellipse. The building itself looks little changed from its original design by James Hoban who based the architecture on country estate houses in Britain and Ireland, but inside it has been completely altered from its original state. The most significant changes include the addition of the Rose Garden in 1913, a third floor for more living space in 1927, and an East Wing in 1942. In 1948 President Truman was forced to move across the street after an examination showed that the building was in a state of serious disrepair. At that time the White House was completely reconstructed within and the balcony on the south portico was also added.

The lights of 16th Street culminate in the great Federalist architecture of the White House. Today the building is in its third century as the symbol of the executive branch of the United States Government.

This photograph of Georgetown looks across the Whitehurst Freeway below the point where it joins the northern end of the Key Bridge, to Georgetown University in the distance. This area of Washington has a rich history. In the 18th century it was a tobacco port populated by wealthy merchants and it also had strong links to the Underground Railroad that helped Southern slaves to flee to freedom in the North.

The Georgetown waterfront. Just out of the photograph to the right Rock Creek empties into the Potomac after winding its way through the park named for it. The creek is often seen as a natural border between the city and Georgetown, which retains its own special character apart from the main city.

Along the Potomac in Georgetown lies the Washington Harbor, a collection of offices, restaurants, and luxury condominiums. One of the city's most desirable addresses, with condos selling for between $550,000 and $5.5 million, it is located just between the Theodore Roosevelt Memorial Bridge and the Key Bridge. The site has become home to the annual Potomac International Regatta.

Georgetown is now home to some of the area's wealthiest citizens and the city's most vibrant nightlife. Its excellent collection of Federal period and Victorian homes make its streets a great place for an afternoon walk. This photograph shows M Street and the Chesapeake & Ohio Canal, which hosts recreated 19th century canal boats for rides in the summer.

Hovering over the Georgetown looking northwest up the Potomac in the early morning. The Key Bridge links Rosslyn, Virginia, to Washington, D.C. and was built on the site of a canal aqueduct and road bridge. The bridge is named after the attorney and amateur poet Francis Scott Key, who wrote "The Star Spangled Banner" and was built in 1923.

Down the Potomac from Georgetown to East Potomac Park are no less than nine bridges. In the foreground is the Key Bridge; cutting across the south of Theodore Roosevelt Island is the bridge also named for that president. A pedestrian bridge links the island to Virginia. Behind the Theodore Roosevelt Bridge is the Arlington Memorial Bridge. In the distance can be seen what looks from this perspective to be a single structure spanning the river but is, in fact, five—the twin George Mason Bridge and Rochambeau Bridge on Interstate 395; the Arland D. Williams, Jr. Bridge; an unnamed bridge carrying Metro subway trains; and the Long Bridge.

Heading north from M Street (the wide boulevard to the left in the photograph) is Wisconsin Avenue (from left to right). Three blocks up and to the west of Wisconsin is St. John's Church, with its distinctive green dome. The church is attributed to the same architect who designed the original Capitol Building—Dr. William Thornton—and has some wonderful art glass windows, including one by Tiffany. The area around the church is noted for its "old world" charm of cobbled streets and (now-unused) streetcar tracks.

The area of Washington known as Georgetown became incorporated in 1789 as George Town. The origin of the name is disputed, some scholars claiming it was named after George Washington, while others proposing that it was named to honor King George II of England. There is also a theory that the city took the name of two of the town's landowners, George Gordon and George Beall.

Founded in 1789 by John Carroll, S.J., Georgetown is the nation's oldest Catholic university. What began as Georgetown College, a small gathering of twelve students and a handful of professors, has grown into a major international university that includes four undergraduate schools, a law school, and a medical school.

The 338 mile-long Potomac River runs through Maryland, Virginia, West Virginia, Pennsylvania, and, of course, Washington, D.C. In the region of 460 million gallons of water are pumped each day from the river to meet the needs of Washington's residents. The reservoir sits on a hillside above the C&O Canal, Canal Road, and the former Baltimore & Ohio Railroad Georgetown Branch, the latter now used as a hiking and bicycle trail.

The Kennedy Center, celebrating its 30th anniversary in 2001, is the nation's busiest arts facility, presenting more than 3,000 performances each year for audiences approaching two million. Two months after President Kennedy's assassination in November 1963, Congress designated the building as a "living memorial" to Kennedy. In December 1965, President Lyndon Johnson turned the first shovel of earth at the site, using the same gold-plated shovel that had been used in the groundbreaking ceremonies for the Lincoln Memorial in 1914 and the Jefferson Memorial in 1938.

This photo shows the Watergate complex, made up of apartments, offices, shops, restaurants, and a hotel, where the most famous political scandal in American history began. On June 17, 1972 a security guard at the complex contacted police when he noticed an unlocked stairwell door. The Democratic National Committee headquarters had been broken into and the scandal would eventually lead to president Richard Nixon's resignation from office.

Theodore Roosevelt Island has a diverse history. Native Americans called the island "Analostan" and used it for fishing. It was later named "My Lord's Island," when King Charles I granted the island to Lord Baltimore. The Mason family owned it for 125 years, operating a ferry from the island to Georgetown. The Masons left "Mason's Island" by 1832, after a causeway built to the Virginia shore stagnated their water. For years after that the island was a picnic resort, except during the Civil War when Union Army troops were stationed here.

The island is now the memorial to America's 26th president. Roosevelt was very committed to nature conservancy: during one impassioned moment he broke from a prepared speech on the subject to declare "I hate a man who would skin the land!" In this shot, you can see the outdoor memorial to the president, with Roosevelt's thought-provoking quotes and a statue that captures the spirit of this forward-thinking leader.

Washington's Dulles International Airport was opened November 19, 1962. Its unique buildings were designed by Eero Saarinen. The airport is named after John Foster Dulles, who was secretary of state under President Dwight D. Eisenhower from 1953-59. It is located about 30 minutes from downtown Washington, in Loudoun and Fairfax Counties in Virginia.

The C&O Canal follows the route of the Potomac River for 184.5 miles from Washington, D.C. to Cumberland, MD. The canal operated from 1828-1924 as a transportation route, primarily hauling coal from western Maryland to the port of Georgetown in Washington, D.C. Hundreds of original structures, including locks, lockhouses, and aqueducts, serve as reminders of the canal's role as a transportation system during the canal era. The old towpath now serves as a bicycle trail for the entire length of the canal to Cumberland.

The site of the Bethesda Naval Hospital (located in Maryland) was chosen by President Theodore Roosevelt. The president's interest was not limited to selection of the site however. He sketched an initial elevation and ground plan (based on the state capital building in Lincoln, Nebraska, which he admired) that French architect Dr. Paul Phillips used as his guide for the design of the center. His distant cousin, President Franklin Delano Roosevelt, laid the cornerstone on Armistice Day, November 11, 1940.

The Temple of the Church of Jesus Christ of Latter-Day Saints is popularly known as The Mormon Temple. The temple was dedicated by Spencer Kimball on November 19, 1974. It took six years to build and measures 160,000 square feet. It is located next to the Capital Beltway in Kensington, a Maryland suburb. Its white marble walls end in six spires. On top of one of these spires is the Angel Moroni, standing 18 feet high. The angel was almost stolen when a thief in a helicopter attempted to lift the statue off of its moorings.

When the Mormon Church decided to build a temple in Washington they realized that such a building would be a symbol of the Church to the government of the United States, and to the ambassadors of the world that lived and visited there. Therefore, the Church decided to build a monumental temple that would be instantly recognizable as a Mormon building. The Mormon temple in Salt Lake City was used as the basis for the new, larger, six-spired temple. The resulting design stopped traffic on the Capitol Beltway until the locals became used to this shining white castle. It often prompts comparisons to the Emerald City in the movie *The Wizard of Oz*.

The David Taylor Model Basin, now part of the Carderock Division of the Naval Surface Warfare Center, was founded over one hundred years ago when the U.S. Navy ranked twelfth in the world and lagged behind every European navy. Today it leads the world in the research and development of undersea vehicle science, ship systems, and related maritime technology. The Carderock Division headquarters is located in West Bethesda, Maryland, ten miles from downtown Washington D.C., just west of the American Legion Bridge carrying the Beltway across the Potomac.

Washington National Cathedral, or the Cathedral Church of Saint Peter and Saint Paul as the Cathedral is formally known, is perhaps the world's last example of a structure built in a purely Gothic style. The Episcopal cathedral is second in size only to New York City's Saint John the Divine. It is built in the shape of a cross and seats about 4,000. The initial design of the building was completed by English architects George Bodley and Henry Vaughan, but American Philip Hubert Frohman is considered to be its principal architect.

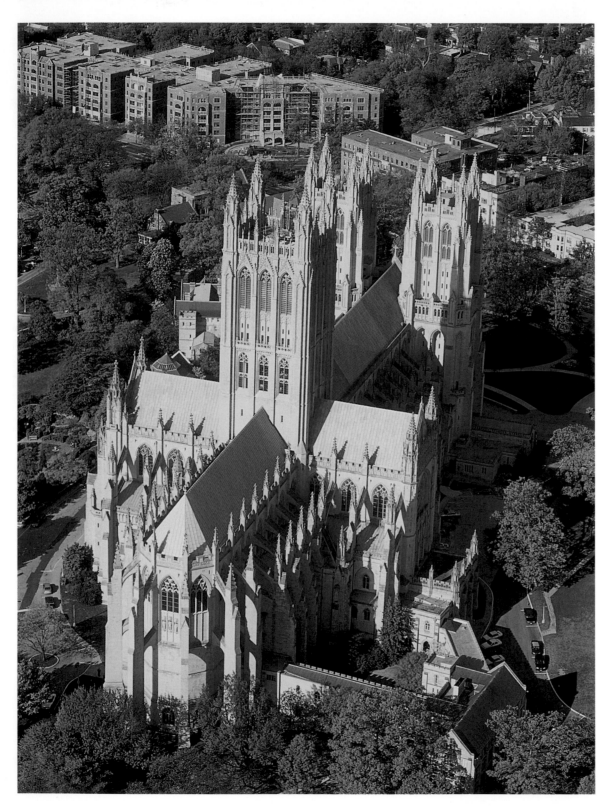

The cathedral sits on 57 acres of landscaped gardens atop Mount Saint Alban, the highest point in the city. Visitors can tour the cathedral, hear free concerts, create brass rubbings, and purchase plants from the greenhouse. Pierre L'Enfant proposed a great national church when he originally drew up his master plan for the city, but it took nearly a century for his idea to be realized. The church's foundation stone was laid in 1907, with President Theodore Roosevelt in attendance. Since then, every president of the United States has attended services or visited the cathedral on a regular basis. The final stone of the cathedral was set on September 29, 1990.

Originally built at 23rd and E streets, NW, in 1844, the Naval Observatory was moved to this site, south of the National Cathedral between Massachusetts and Wisconsin avenues, in 1893. It is an official source for standard time in the United States. In 1904, the observatory broadcast the world's first radio time signals. The Admiral's home, used as the residence of the nation's vice president since 1975, is located in the grounds.

Rock Creek Park is named for the creek it follows for six miles from the Potomac River to the district's Maryland border. It is one of the oldest and largest city parks in the United States, with over 1,754 acres of hills and 35 miles of hiking, biking, and horseriding trails. Just four miles from the White House at its closest, the park gives a rural respite to the city's visitors and residents alike, despite its major roadway being used as a particularly scenic commuter artery on weekdays.

At Rock Creek Park, the area's cultural history can be studied through Peirce Mill (a gristmill where corn and wheat were ground into flour using water power from Rock Creek) and the remains of Civil War earthen fortifications, including Fort Stevens, the site of the only battle within the District of Columbia during the Civil War. This photograph shows the route taken over the park by the Taft Memorial Bridge—named for President William Howard Taft—and Connecticut Avenue just south of the National Zoological Park. Visible to the right is the Duke Ellington Memorial Bridge, which was built in 1934, replacing a streetcar trestle.

The National Zoological Park stretches over a 165-acre wooded area along Rock Creek and is filled with nearly 3,000 different animals representing 900 species. It is part of the renowned Smithsonian Institution and was moved from the Mall to its current location in 1890 by its founder William Temple Hornaday.

In 1972, the Zoo received two giant pandas, a gift of friendship following President Richard Nixon's visit to China. These pandas, Hsing Hsing and Ling Ling, were probably its most famous occupants, visited by nearly three million people each year. Hsing Hsing's death in November, 1999 at the age of 28 elicited messages of sympathy from around the world.

Soon after the zoo was established in 1890, a tradition began which lasts to this day. Families from the city's African-American community come to the zoo on the Easter Monday to picnic, look at the animals, and hunt for Easter eggs. The structure at the center of this photo is the Flight Cage, which houses some of the many birds (including the famous bald eagle) in the zoo's collection. The zoo has worked hard to simulate the natural habitat of each of its animals, and is home to many endangered species.

The National Zoo's exhibits are designed around the BioPark concept. The BioPark aims to break down the barriers between zoos, natural history museums, centers for scientific and scholarly research, and museums of art. In this way visitors can see whole ecosystems—communities of plants and animals living in harmony with their environments. Conventional zoo exhibits often show isolated species in settings far different from the animals' natural habitats and relegate plants to a decorative "supporting role."

The Phillips Collection, at 1600 21st Street NW, calls itself "America's First Museum of Modern Art." Founded by Duncan Phillips in 1930, the collection was originally made up of over 2,000 pieces of artwork collected by Phillips over the course of his lifetime. Phillips' intention was to present a museum of modern art in a domestic setting where he believed "people would be inclined to return once they had found it and to linger as long as they can for art's special sort of pleasure."

Sheridan Circle, like Dupont Circle to its southeast, was named for a Civil War general whose statue stands in its center. It sits on the southern boundary of the Sheridan-Kalorama neighborhood of northwest Washington, which has some of the finest mansions in the city. Built for the city's wealthiest and most powerful families in the 1920s, many of the homes are now elegant embassies. To the upper left, the Dumbarton Bridge curves over Rock Creek and the Rock Creek Parkway to connect with Georgetown.

The Dupont Circle neighborhood contains the city's largest concentration of cafes, bookstores, art galleries, think tanks, embassies, and street performers—plus an impressive array of restaurants, stores, museums, libraries, private clubs, and historic residences. Most of the row houses found in the Circle were built in the 1880s and were originally home to diplomats and professionals, as well as to tradesmen and laborers.

Perhaps the most famous of the city's circles, Dupont Circle was named after Samuel Dupont, a Civil War hero who captured the Confederate port at Port Royal, South Carolina. In 1872, when the area was just beginning its life as a park, it was home to birds given to the city by foreign dignitaries. German and English sparrows made their homes in specially constructed birdhouses placed in the park's tree branches. The German sparrows proved the heartier breed and their descendents now constitute the majority of sparrows seen in the city.

Washington's downtown area extends from Georgetown to Capitol Hill and is extremely lively. Clustered around Connecticut Avenue (at the bottom of the photograph) are many superb restaurants, serving some of the finest cuisine to be found in the city. Further east, toward the Capitol, is the "old downtown" and Chinatown, which also has many fine eateries and bars, but is less expensive than the haute cuisine of the "new downtown."

To the bottom left of this photograph, just off Connecticut Avenue, can be seen the Renaissance-style St. Matthew's Cathedral, the Catholic church that welcomed John F. Kennedy as a frequent worshipper and where there is now a plaque before the main altar which reads, "Here rested the remains of President Kennedy at the requiem mass November 25, 1963, before their removal to Arlington, where they lie in expectation of a heavenly resurrection." Just behind and to the left of the cathedral is the headquarters of the National Geographic Society, which houses Explorers Hall, a free exhibition of expeditions that the society has sponsored over its hundred year history.

Named for the Mexican-American War hero General Winfield Scott, Scott Circle, at 16th Street, Rhode Island Avenue, and Massachusetts Avenue (with 16th Street passing underneath) is one of the city's eight traffic circles in the area (the others include Dupont, Kalorama, Logan, Maine, Sheridan, Thomas, and Washington), all originally designed by Pierre l'Enfant, the city's first master planner.

Looking south from over Scott Circle we can see the view down 16th Street to the White House and, behind it, West Potomac Park, the Tidal Basin, the Potomac, and Reagan National Airport on the far shore. The small Gothic-style redbrick church nestled between two taller buildings just to the left of 16th Street is the Metropolitan African Methodist Episcopal Church, which was once attended by Frederick Douglass, the abolitionist, and was more recently used by President Clinton as the site for both of his inaugural prayer services.

Immediately before the White House is Lafayette Square, named for a young French nobleman, the Marquis de Lafayette, who sailed to America to offer his services in the Revolution and whose statue now occupies the southeast corner. The main statue, visible in the center of the park is of Andrew Jackson. A hero of the 1812 war, who defeated the British at New Orleans, the statue was made from bronze cannons that Jackson captured from the enemy forces. Today the park is an intimate and well tended garden when not populated with protesters, who often congregate there.

The city's nightlife is as diverse and lively as that of any great American city. The theater and performing arts, as well as the live music scene, are absolutely first-rate and a virtual renaissance is taking place in the bar and club scene. Exclusive clubs have also recently appeared in the city, but of course the most exclusive invitation in town still comes from the president himself: dinner at the White House is an invitation rarely refused. The glowing, rectangular building to the left is the National Geographic Building.

Occupied by a statue of Major General George H. Thomas, the Union general of the Civil War after whom it was named in 1879, the circle at the junction of Massachusetts and Vermont avenues and M and 14th streets is a testimony to the original L'Enfant plan for Washington, which envisioned monuments or statues in each public square. The architect recommended that these should be dedicated to great military achievements or to leaders who "were conspicuous in giving liberty and independence to this country."

The scene looking down 14th Street toward Franklin Park. The lights of Thomas Circle can be seen in the foreground of this photograph, which shows the downtown area and the Federal Triangle at night. Washington is not just a place of politicians and monuments. Beneath the surface, and especially at night, it is a thriving 21st century city with a great arts scene as well as comedy clubs, discos, and small venues where every variety of music can be seen from jazz to hip-hop to alternative rock.

Howard University was founded in 1867 just after the Civil War and was named for General Oliver Howard, a Civil War hero and Commissioner of the Freedman's Bureau, which promoted assimilation of freed slaves into society. Early on it achieved widespread recognition as a university committed to educating newly emancipated slaves and their descendants. Today, Howard is the world's largest and most comprehensive university with a predominantly African-American enrollment. In the foreground is McMillan Resevoir, which lies to the east of campus.

Located in north-central Washington, northeast of Howard University in a once rural part of the district, the Soldier's Home—now the U.S. Soldiers and Airmen's home—is a haven of retreat for over 1,300 war veterans. In the late 19th century, it hosted thousands more Civil War veterans.

The Soldiers' Home is one of America's oldest veterans' retirement homes, established in 1851.
Four of the original buildings still stand and are listed as national historic landmarks. Two of
the buildings, Quarters 1 and Anderson Cottage, served as the summer White House for many
U.S. presidents—Chester Arthur, Rutherford B. Hayes, James Buchanan, and most notably
Abraham Lincoln.

The National Shrine of the Immaculate Conception, located on the campus of Catholic University, was completed in 1959. It is constructed in the Byzantine style and is the largest Catholic church in the U.S. and the seventh largest church in the world—Washington National Cathedral is sixth. The church is a spiritual home to hundreds of thousands of pilgrims who journey here each year from every state and many foreign lands.

Established by Congress in 1927, the National Arboretum, along the shores of the Anacostia River in eastern Washington, D.C., is a 446-acre collection of display gardens and historic monuments set among native stands of eastern deciduous trees. Visitors can find something in bloom at all times of the year, but the 70,000 azaleas which flower in the early spring are particularly impressive.

The arboretum contains Japan's bicentennial gift to the United States—a collection of 53 bonsai trees, some of which are over 300 years old. It is the most visited garden collection at the arboretum. Also on display are 22 original neoclassical columns from the U.S. Capitol's East Portico, replaced during a 1958 renovation and stored, forgotten, until they were erected at the Arboetum's Great Meadow for display in 1990.

Across the Anacostia River from the National Arboretum, the Kenilworth Aquatic Gardens are a series of 44 ponds over 700 acres showcasing aquatic plant life of all descriptions. The ponds attract animals as well including frogs, waterfowl, fish, and turtles.

Plans for Kenilworth Aquatic Gardens were included not only in the 1791 L'Enfant Plan for the District of Columbia, but also the McMillan Plan of 1901, which specifically recommended extension of public parkland along both sides of the Anacostia River.

On Florida Avenue, northeast of Union Station, is the campus of Gallaudet University, the world's only university in which all programs and services are specifically designed to accommodate deaf and hard-of-hearing students. It was founded in 1864 by an Act of Congress, and its charter was signed by President Abraham Lincoln.

Union Station was built jointly by the Pennsylvania and Baltimore &
Ohio Railroads on an area of swampland near the U.S. Capitol Building.
The station, designed in the Beaux-Arts style by architect Daniel
Burnham, opened with the arrival of a B&O Railroad passenger train from
Pittsburgh on October 27, 1907. During World War II as many as 100,000
passengers a day passed through the station.

At the time Union Station was built, it covered more ground than any other building in the United States and was the largest train station in the world. The area occupied by the station and the terminal zone was originally about 200 acres. The Washington Monument, if put on its side, could lay within the confines of the Station's concourse. Union Station brought to the nation's capital a new grandeur: 70 pounds of 22-karat gold leaf adorned the 96-foot barrel-vaulted coffered ceilings. The cost was monumental as well—$125 million.

The advent of air travel led to a decline in railroad passengers, and Union Station began to fall into disuse in the late 1960s. An attempt to transform the station into a National Visitor Center failed and the building closed in 1978. It reopened in 1988 having been redeveloped as a bustling retail center and transportation facility.

The northeast of Washington, D.C., which includes the Edgewood, Trinidad, Ivy City, Rosedale, and Isherwood districts, is mainly a residential area dominated to the west by Washington's great monuments and buildings. To the east lies the extensive Anacostia Park, while to the north the city's suburbs roll on into Maryland.

Looking over the northeast part of Capitol Hill, we see the tops of the Supreme Court Building and the Library of Congress, with the Folger Shakespeare Library to the lower right. Also visible are Stanton Park, at the junction of Maryland and Massachusetts avenues; Capitol Hill Hospital, to the right of center; and the Frederick Douglass Home, at 316 A Street NE, former home of the noted abolitionist leader and original home of the Museum of African Art (now part of the Smithsonian complex on the Mall).

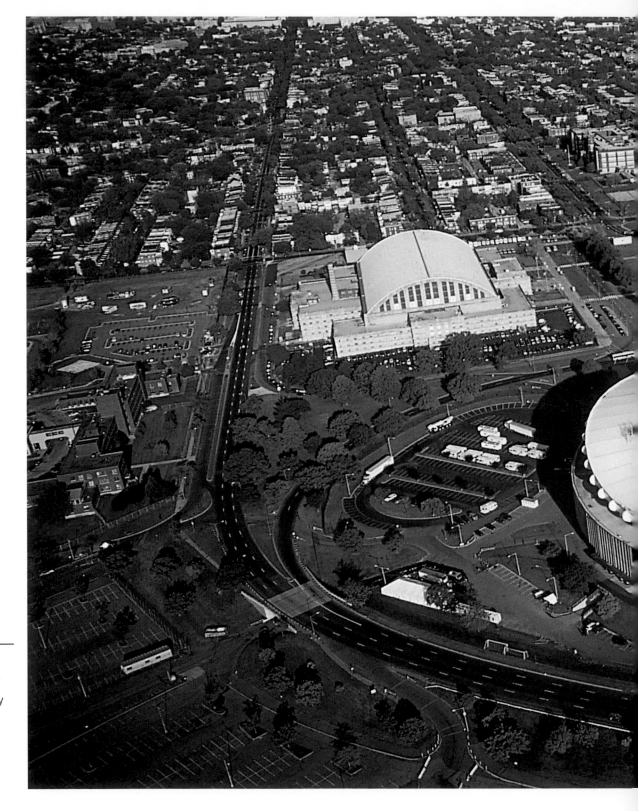

Originally called D.C. Stadium, Robert F. Kennedy stadium was home to baseball's Washington Senators until they departed for Texas and became the Rangers. This 45,000-seat stadium is very modern in its design, circular in shape, with two symmetrical decks for seating. In 1971 the last Major League game played there turned ugly when angry fans stormed the field to protest the Senators' forthcoming move.

The stadium has been Washington's major venue since 1961 (when it was built to replace Griffith Stadium, which was adjacent to Howard University), and hosting pro sports, college athletics, and high school games as well as performances by many of the greatest names in music. The stadium is now the home of D.C. United, Washington's professional soccer team.

The only public hospital in the city, the location of the D.C General Hospital was initially the
relocation site of the Washington Infirmary, the capital's first public hospital established in
1806, when it was moved in 1846. Known as the Washington Asylum it was also used as a
work house for minor criminals. In 1922 a new building was constructed and the facility
received a new name—Gallinger Municipal Hospital—which later became District of Columbia
General Hospital in 1953. To the south of the hospital buildings is the D.C. Jail.

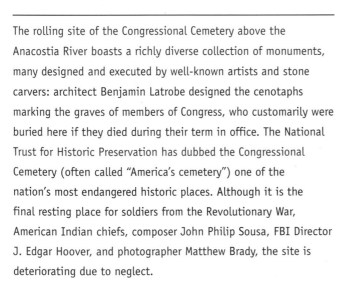

The rolling site of the Congressional Cemetery above the Anacostia River boasts a richly diverse collection of monuments, many designed and executed by well-known artists and stone carvers: architect Benjamin Latrobe designed the cenotaphs marking the graves of members of Congress, who customarily were buried here if they died during their term in office. The National Trust for Historic Preservation has dubbed the Congressional Cemetery (often called "America's cemetery") one of the nation's most endangered historic places. Although it is the final resting place for soldiers from the Revolutionary War, American Indian chiefs, composer John Philip Sousa, FBI Director J. Edgar Hoover, and photographer Matthew Brady, the site is deteriorating due to neglect.

John Philip Sousa Bridge, named after the famous march composer whose compositions are heard every July 4th at Independence Day celebrations across the nation, spans the Anacostia River at Pennsylvania Avenue. The segment of Pennsylvania Avenue it connects to was considered by L'Enfant as the eastern entry to the city.

The Anacostia River flows from Montgomery and Prince George's Counties in Maryland to the District of Columbia, where it empties into the Potomac River and eventually Chesapeake Bay. The river has suffered in recent times from pollution and neglect: it is sometimes called Washington's "forgotten river." Visible on the left side in the distance are St. Elizabeth's Hospital and Bolling Airfield.

Built in 1855 as the U.S. Government Insane Asylum—the name was changed during the Civil War so Union soldiers could be treated there without fear of stigma—Saint Elizabeth's is located in the Anacostia neighborhood of Washington, D.C. and is still in use as a mental institution. Its historic main building, built in the Gothic revival style, is a national landmark. Other highlights of the grounds include "The Point," a soaring hillside with a panoramic view of the nation's capital.

If you are a tourist to the city, do not attempt to visit Saint Elizabeth's. The staff of this active facility are concerned with security and for the safety and privacy of the residents, so the grounds are not open to the public. Unfortunately, the historic old main building is not viewable from the main street.

Navy Yard is the U.S. Navy's oldest shore establishment, in operation since the first decade of the 19th century. It evolved from a shipbuilding center to what is now an administrative center for the Navy. Serving as a gateway to the capital, the yard welcomed the first Japanese diplomatic mission in 1860. Charles A. Lindbergh returned to the Navy Yard in 1927 after his famous transatlantic flight.

Fort McNair sits on the point of land where the Potomac and Anacostia rivers join. It has been an Army post for more than 200 years, third only to West Point and Carlisle Barracks in length of service. The military reservation was established in 1791 on about 28 acres of what then was called Greenleaf Point. The fort has been the headquarters of the U.S. Army Military District of Washington since 1966.

The fort was renamed in 1948 in honor of Lieutenant-General Lesley J. McNair, who was commander of the Army ground forces during World War II. He was promoted to full general posthumously after being killed by friendly fire at Normandy in July 1944. The building in this photograph is the National War College.

This view looking southwest shows the Congressional Cemetery at lower right, with the
Anacostia River spanned by the John Phillip Sousa Bridge carrying Pennsylvania Avenue
between Anacostia and Capitol Hill. The marinas of several boat clubs, including the
Washington Yacht Club and the District Yacht Club, can be seen in the river, as well as
Anacostia Park on the far shore. The railroad line seen bridging the Anacostia River at lower
left is a primary freight railroad line in the Washington area.

Located 12 miles south of Washington in Maryland at the mouth of Piscataway Creek is Fort Washington. The fort was a key site in the defense of the city in the early 1800s. The building that originally stood here was constructed in 1809 (called Fort Warburton), but had to be rebuilt after the War of 1812.

By the end of the 19th century the "Old Fort," as it was commonly known, was rendered obsolete by the "circle forts" erected around the district. After being used for various military purposes, including a military post and a veterans' hospital, it was given over to the Department of the Interior in 1946 to become a park, which it remains to this day. The lighthouse was originally a fog bell tower built in 1882; the light was added to the tower in 1901.

The Pentagon Building serves as the headquarters for the U.S. Department of Defense. It is hard to convey the size of the building: the Capitol building would comfortably fit in just one of its five wedge-shaped sections. It contains 131 stairways, 19 elevators, 284 rest rooms, and 4,200 clocks. Over 200,000 phone calls are made here daily, utilizing 100,000 miles of telephone cable.

It is possible to take a guided tour around the parts of the Pentagon that are not too sensitive, though the guides conduct the tour walking backwards at all times so they can spot anyone attempting to slip away. Highlights of the tour include the Hall of Heroes, where winners of the Congressional Medal of Honor have their names inscribed, many portraits of great military leaders, and scale models of military aircraft and ships.

Arlington Cemetery, perhaps best remembered as home for the Tomb of the Unknown Soldier and the Kennedy Memorial, was for many years the estate of Colonel Robert E. Lee. During the course of the Civil War, this land was seized by the Union Army.

In 1864, with Union dead piling up throughout the Washington area, the search for a suitable site for a military cemetery resulted in a recommendation from Major General Montgomery Cunningham Meigs that Lee's former estate be converted to a burial ground. Meigs, a Southern native, reportedly hated Lee for his service to the Confederate cause. Out of the destruction of the Civil War, and from this personal animosity, was born Arlington National Cemetery.

Robert E. Lee once wrote to a cousin that at Arlington House "my affections and attachments are more strongly placed than at any other place in the world." Today, this house overlooking the Potomac River and Washington, D.C. is preserved as a memorial to General Lee.

The Iwo Jima Memorial, sited just to the north of Arlington Cemetery, captures the famous photograph taken by Joe Rosenthal of five marines and a sailor raising the American flag after one of the most violent battles of World War II. The statue is the largest ever cast in bronze and its inscription reads "In honor and in memory of the men of the United States Marine Corps who have given their lives to their country since November 10, 1775."

Washington National Airport was opened in 1941. Its name was officially changed to "Ronald Reagan Washington National Airport" in February 1998. The airport offers nonstop service to destinations no further than 1,250 miles from Washington, D.C.

In 1946, Ronald Reagan National Airport passed a milestone of one million annual passengers; in 1999, approximately 15 million passengers used the airport with approximately 42,000 passengers a day flying on commercial, general aviation, and commuter flights.

Arlington Memorial Bridge, built between 1926 and 1932, is said by many to be the capital's finest. The adjacent Rock Creek and Potomac Parkway terminus, Watergate steps, and monumental equestrian statuary form a western terminus of the great Washington Mall composition at the edge of the Potomac. The neo-Classical structure is 2,163 feet long and 90 feet between balustrades, carrying a 60-foot-wide roadway and 15-foot sidewalks.

Much of the land seen in this picture was reclaimed from the Potomac River via dredging in the 1800s. L'Enfant Plaza was designed by architect I.M. Pei; opened in 1966, and now includes Federal and private office buildings, an underground shopping mall, and a Metro and commuter rail station. The 10th Street Mall, which terminates at the round plaza at center, includes the Benjamin Banneker Fountain, a memorial to the African-American mathematician. In the foreground is the Washington Channel, the District's waterfront.

The L'Enfant Plaza hotel can be seen in the center of this photograph, just to the left of the Housing and Urban Development Building. L'Enfant Plaza complex rests on the site of the home of Anthony Bowen, a free black community leader who operated a school for African-American children. Bowen also ran an underground railroad station to help convey fleeing slaves to safety in the North. In 1863 he assisted President Abraham Lincoln in recruiting African-Americans from Washington to serve in the Union Army unit called the First U.S. Colored Troops.

The Potomac flowing at dusk past the mouth of the Tidal Basin and the famous cherry trees of Potomac Park. The bridges in the foreground take traffic and rail across the river to the Pentagon. The first bridge at this location, the wood-truss Long Bridge, was built in 1834. It was heavily guarded during the Civil War, and was used as a rail bridge as well after the war. The present rail bridge (at the rear, with a draw span visible behind the subway's rail bridge) occupies the site of the original bridge.

The river is noted for its beauty and there are many scenic trails along its banks for walkers and hikers. The name of the river was recorded by the colonist John Smith and is said to derive from the Native American word "Patawomeck," although the meaning of the word is now lost.

The view over Washington at the end of the day from over the Potomac. The low skyline makes the city seem much more peaceful and dignified from above than places like New York, Boston, or Chicago with their thrusting towers and skyscrapers. Washington, D.C. is in many ways unique, and arguably the most important city in the world, yet it retains the charm of a moderately sized metropolis that has a great many places of interest all within easy distance of each other.

INDEX